THE LITTLE CHOCOLATE COOKBOOK

SUE QUINN

PHOTOGRAPHY BY
YUKI SUGIURA

Hardie Grant

QUADRILLE

CONTENTS

CAKES & BREADS

ARABIAN NIGHTS COFFEE CHOCOLATE LAYER CAKE WITH ROSE-SCENTED GANACHE

SERVES 8-12

The flavours of the Middle East work gorgeously with cocoa - here, cardamom-infused Turkish coffee and the fragrance of Turkish delight in an intense chocolate cake. The result is delicious.

90g/3¼oz unsalted butter,
  plus extra for greasing
250g/8¾oz plain [all-purpose] flour
1½ tsp bicarbonate of soda
  [baking soda]
½ tsp fine sea salt
½ tsp finely ground cardamom
  seeds
200g/7oz dark chocolate (70-75%
  cocoa solids), grated or blitzed in
  a food processor
120ml/4fl oz vegetable oil
400g/14oz caster [superfine] sugar
4 large eggs, lightly beaten
2 tsp vanilla extract
240ml/8fl oz hot strong espresso

FOR THE GANACHE
200g/7oz dark chocolate
  (70% cocoa solids), chopped
250ml/8½fl oz double [heavy]
  cream
20g/¾oz caster [superfine] sugar
½ tsp rosewater

FOR THE COFFEE BUTTERCREAM
150g/5¼oz unsalted butter, softened
300g/10½oz icing [confectioners']
  sugar, sifted
1 Tbsp instant coffee granules
  dissolved in 1 Tbsp boiling water
edible rose petals and/or
  crystallized [candied] rose petals,
  to decorate (optional)

Preheat the oven to 180°C/350°F/Gas mark 4. Butter 2×20-cm/8-in round cake tins and line the bases with baking paper.

Whisk the flour, bicarbonate of soda, salt and cardamom together. Set aside.

Continued...

Melt the chocolate, butter and oil together in a heatproof bowl set over a pan of barely simmering water, making sure the bottom of the bowl doesn't touch the water. Stir to combine, then remove the pan from the heat.

Place the sugar in a mixing bowl or the bowl of a stand mixer, add the melted chocolate mixture and beat with electric beaters or the mixer until well mixed - it might turn grainy, but that's fine. Gradually beat in the eggs and vanilla to produce a smooth shiny batter. Beat in the flour mixture on low speed until just combined. Finally, beat in the hot coffee, giving a final stir with a spatula to make sure all the melted chocolate at the bottom of the bowl is mixed in.

Divide the batter between the prepared cake tins and bake for 35 minutes - check after 30 minutes - until a skewer inserted into the centre comes out clean. Leave in the tins for 5 minutes, then turn out onto a wire rack to cool.

To make the ganache, place the chocolate in a heatproof bowl. Heat the cream and sugar together in a small pan until almost boiling and the sugar has dissolved, stirring so that it doesn't catch. Stir in the rosewater, then immediately pour over the chocolate, stirring constantly until all the chocolate has melted. Leave to cool for 5 minutes, then whisk with a balloon whisk or electric beaters until thick and creamy. This can take a few minutes.

To make the coffee buttercream, beat the butter in a stand mixer or in a bowl with electric beaters until very pale and creamy, then add the icing sugar and coffee and beat until creamy.

To assemble, carefully cut each cooled cake in half horizontally with a serrated knife. Spread the tops of 3 of the cakes with buttercream, then set one on top of the other. Place the un-iced cake on top with its neatest side facing upwards. Finish by spreading the ganache over the top and sides - smoothly or in swirls, as you wish. It should spread very easily, so if it has hardened too much, beat well or melt a little over a pan of barely simmering water. Decorate with edible and/or crystallized rose petals, if using.

PISTACHIO AND NUTMEG CAKE WITH CHOCOLATE AND RASPBERRIES

SERVES 8

Chocolate cakes don't have to be insanely rich and intensely chocolaty. There's nothing wrong with those attributes, of course, but sometimes just a touch of chocolate is in order. This is it: a cake that's decadent, but gently so, with the flavour of the nutmeg bringing out the cocoa notes of the milk chocolate, and tangy raspberries a foil to the sweetness. Adorned with berries, nuts and edible flowers, this is perfect for an elegant summer's afternoon tea.

120g/4¼oz unsalted butter, softened, plus extra for greasing
100g/3½oz shelled pistachios, plus extra, roughly chopped, to decorate
270g/9½oz plain [all-purpose] flour
4 Tbsp cornflour [cornstarch]
2 tsp baking powder
¾ tsp bicarbonate of soda [baking soda]
1½ tsp grated nutmeg
¼ tsp fine sea salt
270g/9½oz caster [superfine] sugar
2 large eggs, lightly beaten
2 tsp vanilla extract
150ml/5fl oz milk
100ml/3½fl oz water
3 large egg whites

FOR THE CHOCOLATE GANACHE
200g/7oz milk chocolate (at least 30% cocoa solids), finely chopped
100ml/3½fl oz double [heavy] cream
pinch of sea salt flakes

FOR THE MASCARPONE CREAM
120g/4¼oz mascarpone cheese
120g/4¼oz crème fraîche
1½ Tbsp icing [confectioners'] sugar, plus extra to taste
150-200g/5¼-7oz raspberries
edible flowers, to decorate

Preheat the oven to 160°C/325°F/Gas mark 3. Butter 2×20-cm/8-in round cake tins and line the bases with baking paper.

Blitz the pistachios in a spice or coffee grinder until fine, being careful not to reduce to a paste. (A food processor won't get them fine enough, but don't worry if that's what you have - the cake will just be a little heavier.) Transfer to a bowl, add both flours, the baking powder, bicarbonate of soda, nutmeg and fine salt and, using a fork or balloon whisk, whisk to combine. Set aside.

Beat the butter and sugar together in a stand mixer or in a mixing bowl with electric beaters until very pale and fluffy - this will take a good 5 minutes. Gradually beat in the whole eggs and vanilla, then beat for a few minutes more. Beat in the flour mixture on low speed in several separate additions, alternating with the milk and water, until just incorporated.

In a scrupulously clean bowl, whisk the egg whites to soft peaks, then gently fold them into the batter. Divide the batter equally between the prepared tins and smooth the tops. Bake for 35-40 minutes until golden and a skewer inserted into the centre of the cakes comes out clean. Leave to cool in the tins for 5 minutes, then turn out onto a wire rack to cool completely.

To make the ganache, place the chocolate in a heatproof bowl. Gently heat the cream until hot but not boiling, then pour over the chocolate. Add the salt and stir until melted and gorgeously thick and shiny. Leave to cool.

For the mascarpone cream, in a stand mixer or a bowl with electric beaters, beat the mascarpone, crème fraîche and sugar together until smooth. Squash one-third of the raspberries with a fork and fold through the mascarpone.

To assemble the cake, spread the tops of both cooled cakes with the ganache, then spread one of the cakes with the mascarpone cream and place the other cake on top, chocolate-side upwards. Decorate the top with the remaining raspberries, chopped pistachios and the edible flowers. Serve immediately.

CHOCOLATE, LAVENDER AND LEMON BUNDT CAKE

SERVES 8-10

The combination of chocolate, lavender and lemon is an absolute
winner in this cake. The lavender is subtle - it's not like nibbling a
bar of Grandma's soap at all - and the lemon adds freshness to the
whole shebang. The cake itself is light and moist, but one best
eaten within a couple of days.

flavourless vegetable oil, for oiling
3/4 Tbsp culinary lavender buds
  (see note on page 14)
350g/12¼oz caster [superfine] sugar
200g/7oz unsalted butter, softened
280g/10oz plain [all-purpose] flour
50g/1¾oz dark chocolate (60-70%
  cocoa solids), grated
50g/1¾oz cocoa powder
1 tsp baking powder
½ tsp bicarbonate of soda
  [baking soda]

½ tsp fine sea salt
3 large eggs
180g/6½oz Greek yogurt
1-2 Tbsp milk, if needed

FOR THE GLAZE
200g/7oz icing [confectioners']
  sugar, sifted
40-50ml/1⅓-1⅔fl oz lemon juice
1½ Tbsp unsalted butter, melted
pinch of fine sea salt
lavender sprigs, to decorate

Preheat the oven to 170°C/340°F/Gas mark 3. Generously brush the inside
of a 2.4-litre/81-fl oz/2.5-quart Bundt tin with oil, making sure to get into all
the crevices.

Blitz the lavender and half the sugar to a powder in a food processor.
Transfer to a mixing bowl or the bowl of a stand mixer, add the remaining
sugar and the butter and beat until very pale and creamy - this will take at
least 7 minutes.

Continued...

Using a fork or balloon whisk, whisk the flour, grated chocolate, cocoa, baking powder, bicarbonate of soda and salt together in another bowl.

In a small jug, whisk the eggs and yogurt together. Add this to the butter and sugar mixture, alternating with the flour mixture, beating well after each addition. Add a splash of milk to loosen if the batter is too stiff to fall off the end of a wooden spoon, but it shouldn't be runny.

Spoon the batter into the prepared tin, smoothing with the back of a spoon to ensure that the batter fills all the crevices at the bottom of the tin. Tap the tin on the work surface a couple of times to remove all the air bubbles. Bake for 40-45 minutes until a skewer inserted into the centre of the cake comes out clean. Leave to cool in the tin for 15 minutes, then turn out onto a wire rack to cool.

To make the glaze, mix the icing sugar, lemon juice, melted butter and salt together in a bowl. Drizzle over the cooled cake so that it covers the top and runs down the sides, then decorate with lavender sprigs.

Note: Culinary lavender is a particularly flavourful variety sold in speciality shops specifically to cook with. Unsprayed lavender buds from the garden are fine, but might vary in strength.

SALVADOR DALÍ-INSPIRED FLOURLESS CHESTNUT, CHOCOLATE AND RUM CAKE

SERVES 8-10

This gorgeously gooey flourless cake was inspired by 'Chocolate with Rum', a recipe in Salvador Dalí's fantastical cookbook *Les Dîners de Gala*. At once a cookbook and an art book, it combines Dalí's wild artistic imaginings with his passion for gastronomy. But food - including chocolate - was an inspiration for his Surrealist images as well as being one of life's great pleasures. His 1930 painting *Chocolate* depicts a woman in the shape of an urn, with chocolate dribbling from her mouth into a cup and onto an apple below. There's nothing surreal about this very rich cake, which makes an excellent and easy dessert.

300ml/10fl oz dark rum
150g/5¼oz pitted prunes
200g/7oz unsalted butter, roughly
  chopped, plus extra for greasing
200g/7oz dark chocolate (70%
  cocoa solids), chopped

200g/7oz caster [superfine] sugar
200g/7oz chestnut purée
3 large eggs, separated
generous pinch of fine sea salt
cocoa powder, for dusting (optional)
cold crème fraîche, to serve

Place the rum and prunes in a pan and bring to the boil, then reduce the heat and simmer gently for 10 minutes. Remove from the heat and leave to cool for at least 15 minutes.

Preheat the oven to 160°C/325°F/Gas mark 3. Butter and line the base of a 20-cm/8-in round loose-bottomed or springform cake tin with baking paper.

Continued...

Melt the chocolate in a heatproof bowl set over a pan of barely simmering water, making sure the bottom of the bowl doesn't touch the water. Remove the bowl from the pan and set aside to cool a little.

Place the butter, sugar, chestnut purée, egg yolks, salt and the prunes with their rum in a food processor and blitz until smooth and creamy. Add the melted, cooled chocolate and blitz again until completely combined. Scrape the mixture into a mixing bowl.

Beat the egg whites in a scrupulously clean bowl with electric beaters or in a stand mixer until stiff but not too firm or dry, otherwise you won't be able to fold them easily into the chocolate mixture. Beat one-third of the egg whites into the chocolate mixture to loosen, then gently and gradually fold in the rest - don't be tempted to beat or you will lose the air. Spoon the batter into the prepared cake tin and smooth the top.

Bake for 1 hour-1¼ hours: when done, the cake should be dry and firm on top (but not springy, as it will be mousse-like in the centre) and coming away from the edge of the tin. Leave to cool in the tin for 10 minutes; it will shrink a bit, but that is as it should be and will firm up a little as it cools. Release from the tin and sit on a wire rack to cool completely.

Dust with sifted cocoa - this isn't essential, but adds a lovely bitter note - and serve with cold crème fraîche.

APRICOT AND BROWN BUTTER CRUMBLE
CAKE WITH CHOCOLATE AND RYE

SERVES 8-10

The tangy floral sweetness of apricots brings a delicious fruitiness to dark chocolate as showcased in the famous Austrian chocolate cake, Sachertorte. Fun fact: during a protracted legal battle in the 1950s and 1960s between Vienna's Hotel Sacher and Demel's patisserie over who owned the original recipe for Sachertorte, apricot jam - and the placement thereof - was the nub of the legal wrangling. While Demel's spreads the jam only under the glossy chocolate icing, Hotel Sacher fills the middle of the cake with it as well. In the end, Hotel Sacher won the right to name its cake the original, but both still serve the confection in their own unique way. There's nothing contentious about this cake - it's unequivocally flavourful and lovely.

125g/4¹/₂oz unsalted butter,
  plus extra for greasing
150g/5¹/₄oz plain [all-purpose] flour
120g/4¹/₄oz dark chocolate (80%
  cocoa solids), roughly chopped
1 tsp baking powder
¹/₂ tsp bicarbonate of soda
  [baking soda]
¹/₄ tsp fine sea salt
160g/5³/₄oz caster [superfine] sugar
1 large egg, lightly beaten
150ml/5fl oz sour cream
300-400g/10¹/₂-14oz fresh apricots,
  halved (and quartered if large) and
  stoned [pitted]

FOR THE CRUMBLE
100g/3¹/₂oz unsalted butter, melted
60g/2¹/₄oz soft light brown sugar
40g/1¹/₂oz caster [superfine] sugar
1 tsp ground cinnamon
¹/₄ tsp fine sea salt
130g/4¹/₂oz plain [all-purpose] flour
25g/1oz ground almonds
30g/1oz breadcrumbs made from
  a dark rye loaf
softly whipped cream, to serve
  (optional)

A couple of hours before you want to make the cake, prepare the brown butter. Place the 125g/4½oz butter in a light-coloured pan and cook over a medium heat, stirring frequently, until it turns dark brown and smells gloriously nutty. Pour into a heatproof bowl and set aside to solidify. (Once it's cooled a little, you can transfer it to the fridge to expedite matters.)

When you're ready to make the cake, preheat the oven to 180°C/350°F/Gas mark 4. Lightly butter a 20-cm/8-in round loose-bottomed or springform cake tin and line the base with baking paper.

Start by making the crumble. Melt the butter. Place the remaining crumble ingredients in a bowl and, using a fork or balloon whisk, whisk to combine, then add the melted butter. Stir with a fork so the butter is completely combined and you have a mixture of large and small clumps. Refrigerate.

For the cake, using a fork or balloon whisk, whisk the flour, chocolate, baking powder, bicarbonate of soda and salt together in a bowl.

Transfer the solidified brown butter to a mixing bowl or a stand mixer, add the sugar and beat together until pale and fluffy - the butter might be a little granular at first, but keep beating and it will turn creamy. Beat in the egg, then the sour cream. Add the flour mixture in several additions, beating on low speed after each one until just incorporated. You don't want to overbeat. Spoon the batter into the prepared tin and smooth the top.

Arrange enough apricot halves (or quarters) on top to cover completely - it doesn't matter which side up, as you won't see them - and push them into the batter a little. Scatter the crumble mixture evenly over the top, making sure it's completely covered. (You might have to break up very large clumps.)

Bake for 1¼ hours until golden on top and a skewer inserted into the centre comes out clean. Leave in the tin for 10 minutes, then run a knife around the edge and release the cake. It's lovely served warm with softly whipped cream.

APPLE AND CHOCOLATE CHIP RYE SHARING SCONE

SERVES 8

Apple and chocolate are flavours that actually work very well
together. You could serve slices of this oversized scone with a
splodge of softly whipped cream on the side, as you would an
individual version. But if you devour some fresh from the oven,
you need nothing more than an appetite.

100g/3½oz cold unsalted butter,
   diced, plus extra for greasing
300g/10½oz plain [all-purpose]
   flour, plus extra for dusting
75g/2¾oz rye flour
50g/1¾oz caster [superfine]
   sugar, plus 2 Tbsp
1½ Tbsp baking powder

¼ tsp fine sea salt
100g/3½oz dark chocolate chips
1 large egg, lightly beaten
125ml/4¼fl oz whole milk
80g/2¾oz crème fraîche
2 medium eating apples
1 tsp ground cinnamon

Preheat the oven to 220°C/425°F/Gas mark 7 and butter a 20-cm/8-in round
springform or loose-bottomed cake tin.

Sift both flours into a mixing bowl, adding the rye bran caught in the sieve
[strainer] back into the bowl. Add the 50g/1¾oz sugar, the baking powder
and salt and whisk with a fork to combine. Rub the butter in with your
fingertips until the mixture resembles coarse breadcrumbs. Fold in the
chocolate chips.

Transfer 1 tablespoon each of the egg and milk to a small bowl or cup and mix
well. Set aside.

Continued...

Mix the remaining egg, the crème fraîche and half the remaining milk together in a small jug or bowl, then stir this into the flour and chocolate mixture. Gradually add enough of the remaining milk to make a shaggy mass, stirring just enough to bring everything together.

Turn out onto a well-floured work surface and, using light hands - by which I mean don't press or squeeze, just touch lightly - briefly knead once or twice, then divide in half.

Lightly roll out one half into a 20-cm/8-in circle. You will need to sprinkle the work surface and rolling pin with flour to prevent sticking. Tuck this disc into the prepared tin.

Peel, core and finely slice the apples, then toss with the 2 tablespoons sugar and the cinnamon. Scatter the apple slices over the dough in the tin. Roll out the remaining piece of dough into another 20-cm/8-in circle and place on top of the apple. Tuck the edges into the sides of the tin.

Brush with the reserved egg and milk mixture and bake for about 25 minutes, or until golden. It's best served warm and eaten on the day it's made.

BLACK SESAME SEED AND
DARK CHOCOLATE BRIOCHE LOAF

SERVES 8

This loaf is similar to Eastern European babka, a plaited loaf filled with chocolate. This one has black sesame seeds in the filling - they work brilliantly with chocolate and impart a more intensely sesame, slightly bitter and smoky flavour. This makes a wickedly good treat for brunch: serve it warm.

FOR THE BRIOCHE
250g/8¾oz strong white bread
  flour, plus extra for dusting
30g/1oz caster [superfine] sugar
7g/¼oz fast-action dried [active
  dry] yeast
½ tsp fine sea salt
3 large eggs, lightly beaten
150g/5¼oz unsalted butter, softened
  and cut into pieces, plus extra for
  greasing
flavourless vegetable oil, for oiling

1 egg lightly beaten with a splash
  of milk, for egg wash

FOR THE FILLING
80g/2¾oz dark chocolate
  (70% cocoa solids), chopped
50g/1¾oz unsalted butter
2 tsp golden [corn] syrup or honey
50g/1¾oz black sesame seeds
40g/1½oz caster [superfine] sugar
15g/½oz cocoa powder
generous pinch of ground cinnamon

To make the brioche, place the flour, sugar, yeast and salt in a stand mixer and stir. Add the eggs. Using the dough hook, mix on low speed for 5 minutes, stopping to scrape down the bowl a couple of times, until the flour is mixed in. Increase the speed to medium and mix for 10 minutes until it is a sticky dough.

Reduce the speed to low and add the butter, a little at a time, adding more once it's amalgamated. When it's all used up, increase the speed to medium and mix for 10 minutes until shiny, elastic and it pulls away from the sides of the bowl cleanly.

Continued...

Butter a large mixing bowl. Tip the dough onto a work surface and press out to form a rectangle about 2.5cm/1in thick. Working left to right, fold one-third of the dough over itself, then do the same with the right side. Repeat with the top and the bottom. Place the dough, seam-side down, in the prepared bowl, cover with plastic wrap and leave somewhere warm for 1 hour.

Tip the dough out onto a surface, gently press into a rectangle and fold as before. Chill for at least 1 hour - it has to be well chilled and firm to work with.

Now, make the filling. Place the chocolate, butter and golden syrup or honey in a heatproof bowl set over a pan of barely simmering water, making sure the bottom of the bowl doesn't touch the water. Stir now and then until melted.

Blitz the sesame seeds in a spice or coffee grinder - they turn to a paste fairly quickly, but that's fine. Add to the chocolate mixture along with the remaining filling ingredients and beat with a wooden spoon until very well combined. Set aside at room temperature to cool completely and firm up a little. Meanwhile, line a baking sheet with baking paper and dust with flour. Set aside.

Once the dough has chilled, roll into a square roughly 30×30cm/11¾×11¾in. Spread with the chocolate filling, leaving a 1-cm/³⁄₈-in border all around. Pull the edge closest to you up and over the filling and roll into a log. Carefully transfer to the prepared baking sheet and refrigerate to firm up for 1 hour.

Using a rolling pin, gently flatten the log into a long rectangle about 30cm/11¾in long and 12cm/4½in wide. Using a sharp knife, cut lengthways into 3×4-cm/1½-in wide strips, leaving 2cm/¾in at the top uncut so that they stay together. Plait the strips, then press the ends together and tuck underneath. Cover loosely with oiled plastic wrap and set aside to rise for 1 hour.

Meanwhile, preheat the oven to 150°C/300°F/Gas mark 2. Brush the loaf with the egg wash and bake for 40 minutes until risen and golden. Serve warm, cut into thick slices.

CHOCOLATE, CHILLI AND LIME CORNBREAD

SERVES 8

This may come as something of a surprise, but chocolate pairs beautifully with the mild, earthy sweetness of corn. This is intended as a sweet cake, but you could also serve it the same way you would conventional cornbread - that is, alongside a spicy chilli or pork carnitas, for example.

FOR THE CORNBREAD
2 Tbsp olive oil, plus extra
  for oiling
180ml/6fl oz natural [plain] yogurt
2 large eggs
60ml/2fl oz lime juice
finely grated zest of 2 limes
200g/7oz cornmeal
70g/2½oz masa flour or plain
  [all-purpose] flour
40g/1½oz cocoa powder

1 tsp bicarbonate of soda
  [baking soda]
75g/2¾oz soft light brown sugar
2 tsp crushed chipotle chillies

FOR THE LIME AND MAPLE BUTTER
100g/3½oz unsalted butter,
  softened
2-3 Tbsp maple syrup
finely grated zest of 3 limes

Generously brush a 20-cm/8-in round baking dish with oil and place in a 200°C/400°F/Gas mark 6 oven to heat up.

Beat the yogurt, eggs, the 2 tablespoons of oil and the lime juice and zest together in a bowl.

In a separate bowl, whisk the remaining cornbread ingredients together with a fork or balloon whisk, then stir the wet ingredients into the dry. Quickly pour into the hot baking dish, smooth the top and bake for about 30 minutes.

While the cornbread is cooking, beat all the lime and maple butter ingredients together in a bowl - electric beaters work best here.

Serve the cornbread hot from the oven with the butter on top.

DESSERTS

CHOCOLATE AND YUZU LAVA CAKES

The love child of a chocolate soufflé and a sponge cake, this
version of a lava cake is filled with curd, and the citrus lends a
fresh, bright note to what really is a very rich dessert. I've used
yuzu, a citrus fruit popular in Japan, because I am obsessed with
its lemon-lime-tangerine zing, and it's now widely available. But
I've also made it with lime juice with lovely results.

The recipe makes more curd than you need, so store leftovers in
the fridge for slathering on toast or swirling into Greek yogurt.

FOR THE YUZU CURD
45ml/1¹/₂fl oz yuzu juice
  (lime juice also works nicely)
100g/3¹/₂oz caster [superfine] sugar
1 large egg
pinch of sea salt
25g/1oz cold unsalted butter, finely
  diced

FOR THE CAKES
150g/5¹/₄oz unsalted butter,
  softened, plus extra for greasing
60g/2¹/₄oz cocoa powder, plus an
  extra 2-3 Tbsp for dusting
90g/3¹/₄oz plain [all-purpose] flour
pinch of salt
120g/4¹/₄oz caster [superfine] sugar
3 large eggs, lightly beaten
3 Tbsp cold espresso coffee
vanilla ice cream or cream,
  to serve

First, make the curd. Place all the curd ingredients, except the butter, in a heatproof bowl set over a pan of barely simmering water. Stir constantly for 15 minutes until thick enough to cling to a wooden spoon; be careful not to overheat the mixture or it will curdle. Using a balloon whisk, whisk in the butter, bit by bit. Carefully take the bowl off the pan and set aside to cool to room temperature, then transfer to the fridge.

Preheat the oven to 200°C/400°F/Gas mark 6. Butter 4 dariole moulds or ramekins with a 160-ml/5½-fl oz capacity, then dust with the 2-3 tablespoons cocoa, tipping out any excess, and place on a rimmed baking sheet.

Using a fork or balloon whisk, whisk the flour, remaining cocoa and salt together in a bowl to combine. Set aside.

Beat the butter and sugar together in a stand mixer or in a mixing bowl with electric beaters until pale and fluffy - this will take a good 5 minutes. Gradually beat in the eggs and then the espresso. Stir in the flour mixture until well incorporated. Fill each dariole mould one-third of the way up with batter. Make a well in the centre of each and fill with a heaped tablespoon of the curd. Cover completely with the remaining batter and smooth the tops.

Bake for 17-18 minutes until risen and springy to touch. Run a knife around the edges of the moulds, then invert onto plates and serve immediately with vanilla ice cream or cream.

SALTED HONEY, PEAR AND
CHOCOLATE TARTE TATIN

SERVES 4-6

Salty caramel, roasted pear, crisp pastry and walnuts fuse into
something completely delicious in this tarte Tatin. The chocolate
surreptitiously enriches the caramel without shouting about it.

1 sheet ready-rolled puff pastry
 or 320g/11¼oz block
plain [all-purpose] flour, for dusting,
 if needed
6 Conference pears (or other small
 pears), about 100g/3½oz each
lemon juice, for squeezing
70g/2½oz unsalted butter, chopped

70g/2½oz caster [superfine] sugar
70g/2½oz runny honey
½ tsp fine sea salt
50g/1¾oz walnut pieces
50g/1¾oz dark chocolate (60%
 cocoa solids), chopped
whipped cream, to serve

If using block pastry, roll out on a lightly floured work surface until 3mm/⅛in
thick. Cut a 23-cm/9-in disc from the pastry, prick all over with a fork and
chill while you prepare the filling.

Peel and halve the pears, then carefully remove the cores with a teaspoon;
you want perfect halves if possible. Transfer to a bowl and toss with a little
lemon juice as you go to prevent browning.

Continued...

Melt the butter in a 20-cm/8-in ovenproof frying pan. Sprinkle over the sugar and cook for 2 minutes until it begins to dissolve, then stir in the honey and salt. Arrange all but one of the pears, cut-side up, in the pan with the narrowest end pointing to the centre - you want them to fit snugly, as they will shrink slightly during cooking. If there is a space left right in the centre, cut a round from the remaining pear half and place it, cut-side up, in the space.

Preheat the oven to 180°C/350°F/Gas mark 4.

Cook over a medium heat for 30 minutes; the butter and sugar mixture should energetically bubble away and reduce down to a thick and syrupy amber-coloured caramel. Shake the pan frequently, and now and then spoon some caramel over the pears.

Remove the pan from the heat and sprinkle over the walnuts and chocolate, filling in any gaps between the pears with the nuts. Cover with the pastry disc and tuck the edges into the sides of the pan with a spoon.

Bake for 30 minutes, or until puffed and golden. Set aside for 5 minutes, then carefully invert onto a plate. Serve immediately with whipped cream.

CHOCOLATE MOUSSE WITH SESAME HONEYCOMB AND OLIVE OIL

SERVES 4

The combination of intense dark chocolate mousse-meets-
ganache with sweet-salty-chewy honeycomb, sesame seeds
and grassy olive oil is outrageously good. Use the very best
chocolate and olive oil you can afford.

FOR THE MOUSSE
150g/5¼oz dark chocolate (70-75%
  cocoa solids), finely chopped
2 large egg yolks
20g/¾oz caster [superfine] sugar
75ml/2½fl oz whole milk
175ml/6fl oz double [heavy] cream

FOR THE HONEYCOMB
40g/1½oz white sesame seeds
1 tsp bicarbonate of soda
  [baking soda]
100g/3½oz caster [superfine] sugar
2 Tbsp golden [corn] syrup
1 Tbsp honey
good-quality extra virgin olive oil,
  rosemary-infused if you have it,
  for drizzling

Start with the mousse. Have the chocolate ready by the hob [stove] in a
heatproof bowl. Whisk the egg yolks and sugar in a stand mixer or in a
heatproof bowl with electric beaters until pale and creamy.

Continued...

Combine the milk and cream in a pan and bring to a simmer. Pour the hot milk over the egg yolk mixture, whisking constantly. Return the mixture to the pan and cook over a medium heat, stirring constantly, for 5-10 minutes until it has thickened to a custard-like consistency: when you lift a wooden spoon out of it, it should stay coated. Pour the custard over the chopped chocolate and stir until melted and glossy, then pour through a sieve [strainer] into a bowl. Cover with plastic wrap, making sure it sticks to the chocolate to prevent a skin forming. Chill for 2 hours, or until set. Remove from the fridge 30 minutes before serving.

For the honeycomb, line a baking sheet with baking paper and have the sesame seeds and bicarbonate of soda measured out and ready by the hob. Place the sugar, golden syrup and honey in a high-sided pan and stir to combine. Set the pan over a medium heat and simmer until the mixture has turned a deep amber colour (a drop spooned into a glass of cold water should turn hard). Remove the pan from the heat and quickly stir in the sesame seeds and then the bicarbonate of soda. Stir constantly as the mixture froths up. Quickly pour onto the prepared baking sheet and leave for about 1 hour at room temperature, or until hard. Break into pieces.

To serve, use 2 dessertspoons to scoop the mousse into oval shapes (quenelles) and place a couple of these in the centre of each serving plate. Sprinkle over some of the honeycomb pieces and drizzle with the olive oil. Serve immediately.

CHOCOLATE, BANANA AND HAZELNUT GALETTE

SERVES 6

Antony and Cleopatra. Meghan and Harry. Gin and tonic. Chocolate
and banana. Some couplings are just meant to be. This is a quick and
delicious dessert you can make from pantry ingredients. Perfect with
a scoop of vanilla ice cream or a cloud of whipped cream on top.

200g/7oz plain [all-purpose] flour
60g/2¼oz caster [superfine] sugar
50g/1¾oz ground hazelnuts
pinch of salt
125g/4½oz cold unsalted butter,
  chopped
2 egg yolks, lightly beaten
2 Tbsp runny honey

100g/3½oz dark chocolate (60-70%
  cocoa solids), roughly chopped
3 medium ripe bananas
1-2 Tbsp demerara [light brown]
  sugar, for sprinkling
1 egg lightly beaten with a splash
  of milk, for egg wash

First, make your dough. Using a fork or balloon whisk, whisk the flour, caster
sugar, ground hazelnuts and salt together in a bowl to combine. Transfer to a
food processor, add the butter and pulse to a breadcrumb consistency. Add
the egg yolks, a little at a time, pulsing between additions, to make a shaggy
dough. Tip out onto a work surface, knead briefly and shape into a disc. Wrap
in plastic wrap and chill for 30 minutes.

Meanwhile, preheat the oven to 180°C/350°F/Gas mark 4 and place a baking
sheet inside to heat. Warm the honey in a small pan and set aside.

Continued...

Roll out the dough between 2 pieces of baking paper into a circle roughly 35cm/14in in diameter. Carefully peel off the top layer of paper.

Using a bowl, plate or pan lid as a guide, mark out (but don't cut!) a circle roughly 22cm/8½in in diameter in the centre of the dough. Using a sharp knife, cut out a circle 32cm/12½in in diameter around the marked-out circle; there should be a 5-cm/2-in border between the marked-out circle and the edge of the pastry.

Scatter the chopped chocolate within the border of the marked-out circle. Thinly slice the bananas and arrange neatly on top of the chocolate. Brush the bananas with the warmed honey and sprinkle with 1 tablespoon of the demerara sugar.

Fold the border inwards, pleating and gently pressing to form a neat edge as you go. Brush the dough with the egg wash and sprinkle with the remaining sugar. Quickly slide the galette on its paper onto the hot baking sheet and bake for 30 minutes until golden and crisp underneath. Serve immediately.

CHOCOLATE, MARMALADE AND GINGER STEAMED PUDDING

SERVES 6-8

Chocolate and marmalade are a magnificent match in this traditional steamed pudding, made more delicious with the addition of nuggets of stem ginger. The sponge itself is lovely and moist, and invested with a generous marmalade crown. But as it doesn't have rivers of sauce, it's best served with a jug of custard - ideally spiked with rum or whisky - alongside.

175g/6oz unsalted butter, softened, plus extra for greasing
5 heaped Tbsp marmalade
50g/1¾oz/3 balls stem [preserved] ginger from a jar, chopped, plus 1-2 Tbsp syrup from the jar, if needed
175g/6oz plain [all-purpose] flour

45g/1½oz cocoa powder
2 tsp baking powder
pinch of salt
175g/6oz caster [superfine] sugar
3 large eggs, lightly beaten
4-5 Tbsp milk
custard or ice cream, to serve

Generously grease a 1.2-litre/42-fl oz/1.3-quart pudding basin [ovenproof bowl] with butter and line the base with a circle of baking paper. Butter a large square of foil.

If your marmalade is very firm, stir in some of the stem ginger syrup; what you want is a loose mixture. Spoon the marmalade into the base of the pudding basin and set aside.

Using a fork or balloon whisk, whisk the flour, cocoa, baking powder and salt together in a bowl.

Continued...

In a mixing bowl or the bowl of a stand mixer, beat the butter and sugar together until pale and fluffy. Gradually beat in the eggs, adding a little of the flour mixture if it starts to curdle. Stir in the flour mixture and enough of the milk to form a soft dropping consistency. Fold in the chopped stem ginger.

Spoon the mixture into the basin and smooth the top. Make 2 pleats in the centre of the prepared foil, place buttered-side down over the basin and secure with string around the rim. Place an upturned saucer in a large pan and place the basin on top. Pour in enough boiling water to come one-quarter of the way up the side of the basin. Cover with a lid and simmer for 1¾ hours, topping up with more boiling water if necessary.

Carefully remove the basin from the pan, then uncover, run a knife around the side to loosen the pudding and invert onto a plate. Serve the hot pudding with custard or ice cream.

CHOCOLATE-SWIRL PAVLOVA WITH ROASTED RHUBARB AND CACAO NIB CREAM

SERVES 6

This version of the classic meringue-topped-with-fruit-and-cream dessert is gloriously gooey and, to be honest, a little messy. The crisp meringue conceals a decadent heart of oozing chocolate, and the rhubarb provides a tangy counterpoint to all the richness.

150g/5¼oz dark chocolate
  (70% cocoa solids), finely chopped
4 large egg whites
200g/7oz caster [superfine] sugar
¼ tsp fine sea salt

FOR THE CACAO NIB CREAM
300ml/10fl oz double [heavy] cream
2 Tbsp cacao nibs

FOR THE RHUBARB
250g/8¾oz rhubarb, cut
  into thumb-sized pieces
40g/1½oz caster [superfine] sugar

Preheat the oven to 120°C/250°F/Gas mark ½. On a sheet of baking paper, mark out a circle roughly 20cm/8in in diameter using a plate or pan lid as a guide. Place on a baking sheet and set aside.

Melt the chocolate in a heatproof bowl set over a pan of barely simmering water, making sure the bottom of the bowl doesn't touch the water. Remove the bowl from the pan and set aside to cool to lukewarm or room temperature.

In a scrupulously clean bowl with electric beaters or in a stand mixer, whisk the egg whites to stiff peaks. Gradually add the sugar and salt, beating constantly until thick and glossy. It's crucial that the mixture is very stiff.

Continued...

Pour the cooled chocolate over the meringue – don't stir or beat it in. Scoop the mixture into the circle marked out on the baking paper to make a neat round, retaining some swirls of chocolate in the meringue. Bake for 1¼ hours until crisp on the outside.

Meanwhile, make the cacao nib cream. Pour 120ml/4fl oz of the cream into a small pan and add the cacao nibs. Bring almost to the boil, then remove the pan from the heat and set aside to infuse and cool.

When the meringue is cooked, remove from the oven and leave to cool. Increase the oven temperature to 200°C/400°F/Gas mark 6. Place the rhubarb pieces in a baking dish, add the sugar and toss together, then spread out in a single layer. Cover with foil and roast for 15 minutes, then remove the foil and cook for a further 5 minutes, or until the rhubarb is tender but still holding its shape. Remove from the oven and leave to cool.

Strain the cooled infused cream and discard the nibs. Whip the remaining cream until it barely holds its shape, then stir in the infused cream.

To assemble the pavlova, top the meringue with the cream and then the rhubarb and any pan juices, and serve immediately.

MANGO CHOC TOPS

For those not in the know, a choc top is a cone filled with vanilla ice cream and enrobed in a shell of hard dark chocolate. That first bite through the shell into the ice cream is always a bit of a killer - tooth pain *and* brain freeze - but always worth the pain. This is a divine update: a tangy mango ice cream with a dark chocolate sauce that 'magically' hardens when it hits the ice cream. Happiness in a cone.

1.1kg/2¹/₂lb ripe mango flesh, ideally Alphonso mangoes (canned or frozen mango pieces also work well)
80g/2³/₄oz icing [confectioners'] sugar, or more if needed
pinch of salt
2 Tbsp lime juice
120ml/4fl oz double [heavy] cream

FOR THE MAGIC CHOCOLATE SAUCE
240g/8¹/₂oz dark chocolate (70% cocoa solids), chopped
2 Tbsp coconut oil (about 30g/1oz)
ice cream cones, to serve

Place all the ingredients for the ice cream in a blender and blitz until smooth. Have a taste: it should be quite sweet and also a little tangy from the lime juice. The balance will depend on the sweetness of your mangoes, so add more sugar if necessary. Chill for 2 hours, then churn in an ice-cream maker according to the manufacturer's instructions.

When you are ready to serve, make the sauce. Melt the chocolate and coconut oil together in a heatproof bowl set over a pan of barely simmering water, making sure the bottom of the bowl doesn't touch the water. Stir to combine, then remove the bowl from the pan and leave to cool a little.

Scoop some ice cream into the cones, pressing it in firmly, then quickly dip the ice cream into the chocolate sauce - and enjoy watching it harden.

DUCK FAT CARAMEL AND
CHOCOLATE BAY LEAF TART

SERVES 8

Banish any notion that this tart tastes like it should form part of the roast dinner instead of the pudding. Using duck fat instead of butter in the caramel imbues all that sweetness with a subtly savoury richness. I've also made this with goose fat, with excellent results. When it comes to how much salt to use in the caramel, that really depends on your personal taste: start with the amount suggested and add more if you like.

FOR THE PASTRY
200g/7oz plain [all-purpose] flour,
  plus extra for dusting
100g/3½oz cold unsalted butter,
  diced
50g/1¾oz icing [confectioners']
  sugar
generous pinch of fine sea salt
2 large egg yolks, lightly beaten

FOR THE CARAMEL
260ml/8¾fl oz double [heavy]
  cream
60g/2¼oz duck fat

270g/9½oz caster [superfine] sugar
75ml/2½fl oz maple syrup
1 heaped tsp sea salt flakes,
  or more to taste
50ml/1⅔fl oz water

FOR THE CHOCOLATE GANACHE
250g/8¾oz dark chocolate
  (60% cocoa solids), grated or finely
  blitzed in a food processor
200ml/6¾fl oz double [heavy] cream
1 Tbsp liquid glucose
3 bay leaves
sea salt flakes, for sprinkling

First, make the pastry. Place the flour, butter, icing sugar and salt in a food processor and pulse to a fine crumb consistency. Gradually add the egg yolks, pulsing between each addition, to make a shaggy dough. Tip out onto a work surface, shape into a disc and wrap in plastic wrap. Chill for at least 1 hour.

Continued...

On a lightly floured work surface, roll the pastry out into a circle large enough to line a 24-cm/9½-in tart tin. Line the tin with the dough: use a ball of excess dough dipped in flour to press it into the fluted sides and to make a neat crease between the edges and base. Gently push some of the excess pastry hanging over the edge of the tin back into the tin - this will allow for shrinkage in the oven. Don't worry if the pastry tears; just patch it up with excess bits of dough. Run a rolling pin over the rim of the tart tin to trim, and pull away any excess pastry. Prick the base with a fork and chill for 20 minutes. Meanwhile, preheat the oven to 170°C/340°F/Gas mark 3.

Line the pastry case with baking paper and fill with baking beans or rice. Bake for 15 minutes. Remove the paper and the beans, then bake for a further 10 minutes until pale gold. Leave to cool in the tin.

Now, make the caramel. Place the cream and duck fat in a small pan and gently heat until the fat has melted. Remove from the heat and set aside.

Place the sugar, maple syrup and salt in a pan with the water and stir to combine. Simmer until the mixture turns a deep amber colour (or until the temperature reaches 150°C/302°F on a sugar thermometer). Remove the pan from the heat and whisk in the cream and duck fat mixture with a balloon whisk - be careful, as it will splutter. Return the pan to the heat and gently simmer, stirring constantly (I use the whisk), until very thick and a rich caramel colour. Pour into the tart case and leave at room temperature to cool and set for 1-2 hours.

To make the ganache, place the chocolate in a heatproof bowl. Place the cream, liquid glucose and bay leaves in a small pan, bring almost to the boil and then remove from the heat. Set aside to infuse for 30 minutes. Remove the bay leaves and reheat until very hot, then immediately pour over the grated chocolate, stirring constantly. Whisk with a balloon whisk or electric beaters until thick and creamy. Spread over the caramel and smooth the top. Sprinkle with sea salt flakes. Serve immediately or leave to set for 2 hours.

FIG AND FRANGIPANE CROUSTADES WITH COCOA AND LAPSANG SOUCHONG SYRUP

SERVES 6

This elegant dessert is based on a recipe in Tamasin
Day-Lewis's excellent cookbook *The Art of the Tart*. In her
version, Tamasin uses pipe tobacco in the syrup, but here we
have smoky notes of lapsang souchong tea instead. It works
a treat, turning a simple tart into something exceptional.

8 large sheets filo [phyllo] pastry,
  each sheet measuring roughly
  30×38cm/12×15in
60g/2¼oz unsalted butter, melted
6 ripe purple figs
caster [superfine] sugar,
  for sprinkling

FOR THE FRANGIPANE
40g/1½oz caster [superfine] sugar
20g/¾oz ground almonds
½ tsp cornflour [cornstarch]
40g/1½oz unsalted butter, softened

FOR THE SYRUP
150ml/5fl oz freshly boiled water
1 lapsang souchong teabag
50g/1¾oz caster [superfine] sugar
1 Tbsp cocoa powder
cream of your choice, to serve

Preheat the oven to 190°C/375°F/Gas mark 5 and line a baking sheet with
baking paper.

First, make the frangipane. Mix all the ingredients together in a bowl to make
a paste and set aside.

Continued...

Lightly brush the filo sheets with melted butter, stacking them on top of each other as you go. Cut out 6×10-cm/4-in circles from the stack using a small bowl as a guide. Transfer to the prepared baking sheet, buttered-side up.

Place about 1 tablespoon of frangipane on each filo circle and spread out, making sure to leave a 1-cm/3⁄8-in border. Thinly slice the figs and arrange, overlapping slightly, on the frangipane, then sprinkle with sugar. Bake for 15-20 minutes until the filo is golden, the bottom crisp and the figs tender.

Meanwhile, make the syrup. Pour the freshly boiled water into a cup, add the teabag and infuse for 2 minutes. Remove and reserve the teabag, then pour the tea into a small pan. Add the sugar and simmer until dissolved, then whisk in the cocoa. Simmer for 7-8 minutes until reduced and thickened to a thin syrup. Have a taste, and if it's lacking lapsang souchong flavour, remove the pan from the heat, pop the teabag in and infuse some more.

Serve the croustades hot with the hot syrup drizzled over and some cream on the side.

COOKIES
& BITES

BROWN BUTTER, BANANA AND TAHINI
CHOCOLATE CHUNK COOKIES

MAKES ABOUT 28 COOKIES

It's hard to think of a more universally adored American
culinary classic than chocolate chip cookies - or one more
fiercely debated when it comes to the 'perfect' version. Chewy
or crisp? Thick or thin? Chocolate chips or gooey chunks?
Galaxies of internet space are devoted to forensic
explorations of the science behind chocolate chip cookie
excellence, and countless recipes lay claim to be the 'ultimate'.

Here's mine: banana, tahini and chocolate make
an outrageously tasty combination.

150g/5¹/₄oz unsalted butter
120g/4¹/₄oz plain [all-purpose] flour
120g/4¹/₄oz spelt flour
³/₄ tsp baking powder
¹/₂ tsp bicarbonate of soda
  [baking soda]
¹/₂ tsp fine sea salt
280g/10oz dark chocolate (70%
  cocoa solids), roughly chopped,
  with some biggish chunks and
  some small bits

1 very ripe banana, about
  100g/3¹/₂oz without skin
1 large egg
220g/7³/₄oz soft light brown sugar
40g/1¹/₂oz granulated sugar
1 tsp vanilla extract
80g/2³/₄oz tahini (must be smooth
  and runny enough to run off a
  spoon easily - see page 91)
sea salt flakes or fleur de sel,
  for sprinkling

Place the butter in a heavy, light-coloured pan and melt over a medium-high heat, swirling frequently, until the butter smells gorgeously nutty and has turned dark brown. Remove from the heat and transfer to a mixing bowl or the bowl of a stand mixer, making sure you scrape in all the brown bits from the bottom of the pan (this is flavour!). Leave to cool for at least 5 minutes.

Meanwhile, using a fork or balloon whisk, whisk the flours, baking powder, bicarbonate of soda and salt together in a bowl to combine. Add the chopped chocolate and stir to evenly distribute.

In a small bowl, mash the banana until smooth, then add to the cooled butter along with the egg, both the sugars, vanilla and tahini. Whisk for a good 5 minutes until creamy and much paler than when you started - this is a sign that the mixture has aerated well.

Fold in the flour and chocolate mixture in 2 additions. Don't overmix or beat smooth; dough with an uneven consistency delivers welcome texture to the baked cookies. Chill for at least 2 hours.

Preheat the oven to 170°C/340°F/Gas mark 3 and line a large baking sheet with baking paper (you will need to cook these in batches). Scoop heaped tablespoons of dough onto the prepared baking sheet (about 40-45g/1½-1¾oz each), leaving at least 5cm/2in between them. Bake for 6 minutes, then turn the baking sheet round and bake for a further 6 minutes or so until brown at the edges (the centre might look a little undercooked, but it's not).

Lightly sprinkle the cookies with the sea salt while still warm. Leave on the baking sheet for 5 minutes, then transfer to a wire rack to cool.

CHOCOLATE-DIPPED ORANGE
AND CARAWAY SHORTBREAD

MAKES 12 SHORTBREADS

Shortbread, generally, is delicious in its plain simplicity, but in this version, caraway adds vibrant flavour. It can be a pungent spice with a strong earthy taste and notes of aniseed, black pepper and citrus, but used with a light hand as it is here, it lends a gentle perfume to the soft buttery shortbread, and chimes beautifully with the orange zest. It also teases out the cocoa flavours in the milk chocolate - very moreish.

335g/11¾oz unsalted butter, softened
finely grated zest of 2 large oranges
120g/4¼oz icing [confectioners'] sugar
300g/10½oz plain [all-purpose] flour

75g/2¾oz cornflour [cornstarch]
3 tsp caraway seeds
generous ¼ tsp fine sea salt
300g/10½oz milk chocolate, finely chopped

Preheat the oven to 150°C/300°F/Gas mark 2. Line the base and sides of a 20×20-cm/8×8-in brownie tray or baking dish with baking paper, cutting slits in each corner so that it fits neatly. Let the paper hang over the edges so that you can use it as handles to lift the cooked shortbread out of the tray.

Beat the butter and orange zest together in a stand mixer or in a mixing bowl with electric beaters until pale and creamy - this will take a good 5 minutes. Gradually beat in the icing sugar.

Continued...

In a separate bowl, using a fork or balloon whisk, whisk both flours, the caraway seeds and salt together. Add to the butter mixture and beat on low speed until the flour is only just combined. Don't overbeat or the shortbread will be tough. Press the mixture evenly into the prepared tray or dish and bake for 50-55 minutes until firm and the palest gold. Leave in the tray or dish to cool completely.

When cool, lift out onto a chopping [cutting] board. You can cut the shortbread into whatever size pieces you like, but this is the way I like to do it. Using a serrated knife, slice the shortbread square in half and then cut each half into 6 fingers, roughly 10×3cm/4×1¼in. The pieces might crumble, but this is the nature of shortbread - we're not aiming for diamond-cut edges here. Transfer to a wire rack set over a rimmed baking sheet or board.

Melt the chocolate in a heatproof bowl set over a pan of barely simmering water, making sure the bottom of the bowl doesn't touch the water. Spoon the chocolate over half of each shortbread finger. Leave to set at room temperature for at least 1 hour.

RYE CHOCOLATE BROWNIE AND
PEANUT BUTTER COOKIE SANDWICHES

The genius behind Reese's Peanut Butter Cups was one Harry
Burnett (H.B.) Reese, a former employee of US chocolate scion
Milton S. Hershey. Reese set out to make his own name in the candy
business in the 1920s and his peanut butter chocolate bites were an
immediate hit. Little wonder really, at least to those of us for whom
these morsels are catnip; the sweetened peanut butter nestled in a
chocolate case embodies the holy trinity of fat, sugar and salt. Why
not make these luscious cookie sandwiches in honour of Reese.

FOR THE COOKIES
120g/4¼oz unsalted butter, softened
180g/6½oz soft light brown sugar
1 large egg, lightly beaten
1 tsp vanilla extract
125g/4½oz cocoa powder
35g/1¼oz plain [all-purpose] flour
35g/1¼oz rye flour
½ tsp bicarbonate of soda
 [baking soda]
½ tsp fine sea salt

FOR THE FILLING
130g/4½oz smooth peanut butter
25g/1oz unsalted butter
40g/1½oz icing [confectioners']
 sugar, sifted
pinch of salt, if needed

Preheat the oven to 160°C/325°F/Gas mark 3 and line a large baking sheet with baking paper. You will probably have to cook these cookies in a couple of batches.

Beat the butter and sugar together in a stand mixer or in a mixing bowl with electric beaters until pale and creamy - this will take a good 5 minutes. Gradually add the egg and then the vanilla.

Using a fork or balloon whisk, whisk the cocoa, both flours, bicarbonate of soda and salt together in a bowl. Add to the butter mixture in 3 or 4 additions, beating on low speed after each, but only just enough to incorporate the flour - overbeating could make the cookies tough.

Roll tablespoons of the mixture into balls, about 15g/½oz each, and arrange on the prepared baking sheet with a 5-cm/2-in gap between them. Flatten with your palm to make discs 3cm/1¼in in diameter.

Bake for about 8 minutes. The cookies will be soft but will firm up as they cool. Leave on the baking sheet for 5 minutes, then transfer to a wire rack to cool completely. Repeat with the rest of the mixture.

While the cookies are cooling, beat all the filling ingredients together in a bowl with electric beaters or stand mixer until creamy and smooth, adding salt to taste (this will depend on the saltiness of the peanut butter you use). Chill until needed.

When the cookies are completely cool, spread some of the filling over the smooth side of one cookie, then sandwich another one on top. Repeat with the rest of the filling and cookies.

BEEF AND CHOCOLATE PIES ('MPANATIGGHI)

MAKES 16

Legend has it that these extraordinary morsels were invented in
the 1600s by nuns of the Origlione monastery in Palermo, as a
surreptitious way to partake of meat during Lent, when it was
forbidden. Another theory suggests that making the pies was a way
to preserve meat in times of abundance. What is certain is there's
nothing meaty at all about them, and they're heavenly eaten warm.

FOR THE PASTRY
350g/12¼oz plain [all-purpose]
  flour, plus extra for dusting
90g/3¼oz icing [confectioners']
  sugar, plus extra, sifted, for dusting
100g/3½oz cold lard or butter
4 large egg yolks, lightly beaten
100ml/3½fl oz cold water

FOR THE FILLING
65g/2¼oz good-quality lean beef,
  finely chopped (not ready-bought
  mince/ground beef)
70g/2½oz ground almonds
75g/2¾oz caster [superfine] sugar
10g/⅓oz cocoa powder
25g/1oz dark chocolate (about
  70% cocoa solids), grated
1 tsp ground cinnamon
2 large egg whites

Start with the pastry. Using a fork or balloon whisk, whisk the flour and icing
sugar together in a bowl to combine. Grate in the lard or butter and rub it in
with your fingertips until you have small pieces of fat - maybe slightly larger
than grains of rice - coated in flour. Stir in the egg yolks, then add the cold
water, a little at a time, stirring to bring the mixture together into a scraggy
dough. Knead lightly in the bowl until smooth, then shape into a disc, wrap in
plastic wrap and chill for at least 1 hour.

Continued...

Now, make the filling. Fry the beef in a dry frying pan, moving the meat around constantly, until browned. Set aside to cool for 5 minutes. Place the remaining ingredients in a food processor, add the cooled meat and blitz to a paste. Scrape into a small bowl and chill until needed.

When you're ready to make the pies, preheat the oven to 180°C/350°F/Gas mark 4 and line 1 large or 2 small baking sheets with baking paper. Roll out the dough on a lightly floured work surface to 3mm/⅛in thick. Using a 10-cm/ 4-in cutter or small bowl, cut out 16 rounds and transfer to the prepared baking sheet as you go.

Place 1 level tablespoon of the filling in the centre of each pastry circle. Lightly brush the edges with water and fold the pastry over the filling. Gently press around the filling with your thumbs to remove any air pockets, then lightly press the pastry layers together to seal.

Trim the pies using a cutter roughly 7cm/2¾in in diameter - I use a fluted cookie cutter, but you could use a glass dipped in flour. Place the cutter over the half-moon-shaped pies so that the filling is roughly in the centre. Press down to cut away the excess pastry, making sure not to cut into the filling, and to leave a sealed edge all the way around. Using scissors, snip the top of each pastry to make a small air hole.

Bake for 15 minutes, or until the bottoms of the pies are pale gold. The tops will be firm but not brown. Leave to cool a little and dust with icing sugar before serving.

PASSIONFRUIT AND ORANGE CURD TARTLETS
WITH SUMAC AND CHOCOLATE

MAKES 6 LITTLE TARTLETS

Sometimes unlikely chocolate pairings work extremely well, and thus it is with sumac, a pretty purple spice grown in the Middle East and the Mediterranean. Actually, it's not surprising that the combination works, as ground sumac has a tangy lemon flavour and chocolate pairs beautifully with citrus. There's only a little used here, but it really adds a zingy hint of fruitiness to the chocolate. You will need 6×10-cm/4-in loose-bottomed tartlet tins.

FOR THE CURD
10 large passionfruit, yielding about
   165g/5³⁄₄oz pulp
finely grated zest of 1 large orange
100g/3¹⁄₂oz unsalted butter, melted
   and cooled a little
100g/3¹⁄₂oz caster [superfine] sugar
2 large eggs plus 2 egg yolks,
   lightly beaten

FOR THE PASTRY
195g/7oz plain [all-purpose] flour,
   plus extra for dusting

120g/4¹⁄₄oz very cold unsalted
   butter, chopped
30g/1oz caster [superfine] sugar
1 tsp white wine vinegar
¹⁄₄ tsp fine sea salt
about 50ml/1²⁄₃fl oz cold water

FOR THE CHOCOLATE
180g/6¹⁄₂oz dark chocolate
   (60% cocoa solids), chopped
1¹⁄₂ tsp sumac

Start with the curd. Halve the passionfruit and scoop the pulp into a small pan, then warm through. Don't let it boil; a little heat just makes it easier to separate out the seeds. Push the pulp through a sieve [strainer] set over a heatproof bowl (one that will sit over a pan) using the back of a spoon, then scrape the pulp from the underside of the sieve until all you have left are seeds. Add the remaining curd ingredients to the bowl and stir to combine.

Continued...

Set the bowl over a pan of barely simmering water and stir constantly - I stir with a balloon whisk - until the mixture thickens to a custard-like consistency. This will take around 10 minutes. Transfer to a bowl, cover with plastic wrap so that it touches the curd to prevent a skin forming and leave to cool completely, or chill overnight for the best results.

To make the pastry, place all the ingredients, except the water, in a food processor and pulse to a breadcrumb consistency. Add the water gradually until the mixture comes together into a ball. Turn out onto a lightly floured work surface, knead briefly, then shape into a disc and chill for at least 2 hours. Get your 6×10-cm/4-in loose-bottomed tartlet tins ready.

Roll out the pastry on a lightly floured work surface to 3mm/⅛in thick. Cut out 6×14-cm/5½-in circles using a plate or bowl as a guide. Place a pastry circle centrally over one of the tartlet tins and gently press it in with your fingers. Use an offcut of pastry rolled into a ball and dipped in flour to gently push the pastry into the fluted sides of the tin, and into the edge where the sides meet the base. You should have an overhang of pastry all around, so gently push the excess back into the tin to reinforce the edge - this will allow for shrinkage in the oven. Repeat with the rest of the dough circles and tins, then chill for 20 minutes.

Meanwhile, preheat the oven to 170°C/340°F/Gas mark 3.

When the pastry cases have chilled, line them with a double layer of foil and fill with baking beans or rice. Bake for 20 minutes, then remove the foil and beans and bake for a further 5-10 minutes. Leave to cool in their tins.

Melt the chocolate in a heatproof bowl set over a pan of barely simmering water, making sure the bottom of the bowl doesn't touch the water. Stir in the sumac. Spoon about 25g/1oz of the chocolate into each cooled pastry case, spread over the base and leave to set. Stir the passionfruit curd to loosen and spoon over the set chocolate. Serve immediately.

PISTACHIO, CITRUS AND
DARK CHOCOLATE CINNAMON ROLLS

MAKES 7 ROLLS

Like the Black Sesame Seed and Dark Chocolate Brioche Loaf on page 24, these rolls make a decadent brunch, served warm from the oven, with a pot of good strong coffee on the side.

FOR THE DOUGH
240ml/8fl oz whole milk
50g/1¾oz unsalted butter, cut into pieces, plus extra for greasing
400g/14oz strong white bread flour, plus extra for dusting
7g/¼oz fast-action dried [active dry] yeast
¾ tsp fine sea salt
1 large egg, lightly beaten
flavourless vegetable oil, for oiling
1 egg yolk, lightly beaten, for brushing

FOR THE FILLING
80g/2¾oz pistachios, finely chopped
115g/4oz soft dark brown sugar
1 tsp ground cinnamon
80g/2¾oz dark chocolate (70-80% cocoa solids), chopped
50g/1¾oz chopped mixed candied citrus peel
80g/2¾oz unsalted butter, softened

To make the dough, heat the milk in a small pan until almost boiling. Remove the pan from the heat, add the butter and stir until completely melted. Set aside to cool to lukewarm.

Continued...

Meanwhile, in a mixing bowl or the bowl of a stand mixer, whisk the flour, yeast and salt together with a fork or balloon whisk. Add the whole beaten egg and then the lukewarm milk. Knead with a dough hook attachment for 5 minutes, or turn out onto a lightly floured work surface and knead by hand for 8-10 minutes. The dough will be quite sticky at first, but becomes smooth and elastic as you knead - add a little more flour if it's too wet to work with.

Place the dough in a large lightly oiled bowl (it will expand considerably) and turn over to coat. Cover with a clean tea [dish] towel and set aside somewhere warm for 1 hour, or until doubled in size.

While you're waiting, mix all the filling ingredients, except the butter, together in a bowl. Butter a 23-cm/9-in round loose-bottomed or springform cake tin with sides at least 5cm/2in high. Wrap the base in foil, as the filling sometimes melts and seeps out a little.

When the dough has risen, press down on it to let the air out and tip out onto a lightly floured work surface. Roll into a rectangle roughly 35×25cm/14×10in, making sure the middle is no thicker than the edges. With the long side of the dough parallel to the edge of your work surface, spread the butter evenly over the top. Sprinkle over the filling and press down on it gently. Working with the long side, carefully roll the dough into a sausage shape, like a Swiss [jelly] roll.

Cut into 7 equal pieces, each about 5cm/2in long, and arrange, cut-side up, in the prepared tin: place one roll in the centre and the others around it, with a little space in between. Cover with a clean tea towel and set aside for 30 minutes. Meanwhile, preheat the oven to 180°C/350°F/Gas mark 4.

Brush the tops of the rolls with the beaten egg yolk and bake for 20-25 minutes until golden on top. Leave in the tin for 5 minutes, then release and pull apart when cool enough to handle. These are delicious served warm, but will keep well in an airtight container for a couple of days.

CHOCOLATE BRIOCHE DOUGHNUTS WITH BAY CARAMEL CUSTARD AND NIB SUGAR

MAKES 12 DOUGHNUTS

Making these beauties is a project, without question, but they require far less effort than you might think. The most time-consuming part is waiting for the dough to rise and prove, so you can mostly go about your business, but with a little skip in your step at the prospect of truly lovely doughnuts. The subtle savoury flavour of bay partners beautifully with caramel and chocolate.

FOR THE CHOCOLATE BRIOCHE
220g/7³⁄₄oz strong white bread flour
30g/1oz cocoa powder
30g/1oz caster [superfine] sugar
7g/¹⁄₄oz fast-action dried [active dry] yeast
¹⁄₄ tsp fine sea salt
3 large eggs, lightly beaten
125g/4¹⁄₂oz unsalted butter, softened (but not too soft), cut into small pieces
flavourless vegetable oil, for oiling
about 1.5 litres/50fl oz vegetable oil, such as sunflower or rapeseed [canola], for deep-frying

FOR THE BAY CARAMEL
3 medium-large dried bay leaves
70g/2¹⁄₂oz caster [superfine] sugar
50ml/1²⁄₃fl oz double [heavy] cream
35g/1¹⁄₄oz unsalted butter, chopped
2 Tbsp water
generous pinch of sea salt flakes

FOR THE CUSTARD
80ml/2³⁄₄fl oz whole milk
45ml/1¹⁄₂fl oz double [heavy] cream
2 egg yolks, lightly beaten
25g/1oz caster [superfine] sugar
15g/¹⁄₂oz cornflour [cornstarch]

FOR THE NIB SUGAR
10g/¹⁄₃oz cacao nibs
65g/2¹⁄₂oz caster [superfine] sugar
1 heaped tsp ground cinnamon
pinch of fine sea salt

First, make the brioche. Place the flour, cocoa, sugar, yeast and salt in a stand mixer and stir to combine. Add the eggs. Using the dough hook attachment, mix on low speed for 5 minutes, stopping to scrape down the bowl a couple of times, until all the flour is incorporated. Increase the speed to medium and mix for 10 minutes.

Reduce the speed to low and add the butter, a few pieces at a time. When the butter is all used up, increase the speed to medium and mix for a further 10 minutes, or until the dough is shiny, elastic and comes away from the sides of the bowl cleanly.

Tip the dough out onto a work surface and press out to form a rectangle about 1cm/⅜in thick. Fold one-third of the dough over onto itself, then do the same with the other side. Repeat with the top and the bottom. Place the dough, seam-side down, in a large oiled bowl - the dough needs space to expand - cover with oiled plastic wrap and set aside somewhere warm for an hour or so until doubled in size.

Meanwhile, line a large baking sheet with baking paper. When the dough has risen, press your hand into it to release some air and break off about 12×45-g/1½-oz pieces, about the size of a large golf ball. Gently flatten on your work surface, then bring the edges together into the middle, holding them in place with your thumb. Turn the dough over so that the join is at the bottom. Cup your hand over the dough and, using firm pressure, roll on the work surface to make a smooth tight ball. Transfer to the prepared baking sheet and repeat with the rest of the dough, leaving a 3-cm/1¼-in space between each ball. Cover with oiled plastic wrap and set aside for about 1 hour, or until increased in size by 50 per cent. (The time this takes depends on how warm your kitchen is.)

While this is happening, make the bay caramel custard. Place the bay leaves and a few spoonfuls of the sugar in a spice or coffee grinder and blitz to a powder. Mix with the rest of the sugar.

Have the cream and butter ready by the hob [stove]. Place the sugar and water in a small pan, stir to combine and set over a medium heat. Bring to a simmer, swirling the pan now and then (don't stir) until the sugar has dissolved. Simmer until the mixture turns a deep amber colour. Remove from the heat and stir in the cream - beware, as it will splatter - and then stir in the butter and salt. Set the caramel aside.

For the custard, place the milk and cream in a small pan. Bring almost to the boil, then remove from the heat. In a bowl, stir the egg yolks, sugar, cornflour and just enough of the hot milk mixture together to make a very loose paste. Gradually stir in the rest of the milk, then transfer the lot back into the pan. Cook over a gentle heat, stirring constantly, until thickened. Don't let it boil. Remove from the heat and stir in the caramel, then return the pan to a gentle heat, stirring, until thick. Don't let the mixture get too hot or it will separate and use a balloon whisk if needed to remove any lumps. Transfer to a disposable piping bag, fasten closed with a clip and leave to cool completely.

To make the nib sugar, finely grind the cacao nibs to a powder in a spice or coffee grinder. Combine with the sugar, cinnamon and salt and place in a shallow bowl.

To fry the doughnuts, place enough oil in a large heavy pan (a cast-iron casserole [Dutch oven] is perfect) to come 5cm/2in up the sides and heat to 170-180°C/340-350°F. Have a wire rack lined with paper towels by the side of the hob.

Lower 2 or 3 doughnuts at a time into the hot oil. Fry for about 1 minute on each side until puffed up and golden. It's important to keep adjusting the temperature - or even remove the pan from the heat - now and then, to ensure the oil doesn't get too hot or cool. Remove the cooked doughnuts with a slotted spoon to the wire rack.

While the doughnuts are still warm, cut a slit in the side of each and pipe in a generous amount of the caramel custard, then roll in the nib sugar. They are best eaten warm.

BITS & PIECES

WHIPPED MEXICAN-STYLE HOT CHOCOLATE WITH CINNAMON AND ALMONDS

MAKES ENOUGH FOR 6 CUPS

This is a simpler version of traditionally made Mexican hot chocolate. For an extra-special touch, try to get hold of the molinillo - a type of wooden whisk used to froth up the chocolate. The dry mix keeps well in a sealed jar inside a cool cupboard.

140g/5oz dark chocolate (about 70% cocoa solids), broken into pieces
1 tsp ground cinnamon
2 heaped tsp flaked [slivered] almonds
2¹/₂ Tbsp soft light brown sugar
good pinch of sea salt flakes

TO SERVE
whole milk
chilli [red pepper] flakes

Place all the ingredients for the chocolate mix in a food processor and blitz to a fine rubble - don't overdo it or the chocolate will melt and turn into a paste.

Heat the milk in a pan almost to boiling point, then remove from the heat and add 3 tablespoons for each 250ml/8¹/₂fl oz of milk used. Whisk or beat to a lovely froth. Serve with a pinch of chilli flakes on top.

CHOCOLATE AND CHILLI POPCORN

SERVES 4 PER BATCH

If you are feeding a crowd, you might want to make several batches
of these addictive morsels, but this is a good amount to cook at one
time, so as not to burn the popcorn.

50g/1¾oz popcorn kernels
2 Tbsp vegetable oil (olive oil is fine)
50g/1¾oz caster [superfine] sugar
2 Tbsp liquid glucose
3 Tbsp cocoa powder
60g/2½oz unsalted butter

¼ tsp vanilla extract
⅛ tsp (generous pinch of) sea salt
  flakes
⅛ tsp (generous pinch of) hot ancho
  or other chilli powder

Preheat the oven to 120°C/250°F/Gas mark ½ and line a rimmed baking sheet
with baking paper. Place the corn kernels and oil in a heavy, lidded pan, large
enough to fit the kernels easily in one layer. Stir to coat in the oil, set the pan
over a medium-high heat and cover. As soon as you hear the kernels start to
pop, wearing oven gloves, carefully give the pan a good shake, up and down
while holding the lid on. Return to the heat and cook, shaking now and then,
until the corn stops popping. Transfer the popcorn to a heatproof bowl.

Place the sugar, liquid glucose, cocoa and butter in a small pan over a
medium heat and stir until the butter melts and the sugar dissolves. Simmer
very gently for 1 minute; the mixture will thicken slightly and turn to caramel.
Remove from the heat and stir in the vanilla.

Pour the chocolate over the popcorn, then using a rubber spatula, mix well.
Spread out in a single layer on the prepared baking sheet, pressing down
to flatten any clumps. Sprinkle with the salt and chilli powder. Bake for
30 minutes, stirring several times. Remove from the oven and allow to cool to
room temperature. Break into small clumps and store in an airtight container.

CHOCOLATE BARK

This isn't a recipe as such, rather a guide to making shards of beautifully decorated chocolate. Before you start, decide what toppings you would like to decorate your bark with, and have them ready, as you need to add them before the melted chocolate sets.

600g/21oz dark chocolate (no more than 70% cocoa solids), chopped

TOPPING IDEAS
seeds
salt crystals, crushed peppercorns and chilli [red pepper] flakes
freeze-dried fruits and powders, especially raspberry, strawberry and passionfruit
chopped nuts, including green pistachios for vibrant colour
dried edible flowers for texture and colour, such as cornflowers, rose and calendula

chopped dried fruit, including unusual ones such as barberries and dried cranberries
chopped stem [preserved] ginger and crystallized [candied] fruit
savoury morsels, such as chopped pretzels, crackers and potato crisps
chopped sweet cookies and biscuits
toasted sourdough breadcrumbs or toasted coconut flakes
chopped sweets [candies] and sprinkles, such as liquorice allsorts, Smarties and marshmallows

Butter a large rimmed baking sheet or roasting tray and line with baking paper - the butter will help it stay in place. Slowly melt the chopped chocolate in a heatproof bowl set over a pan of barely simmering water, making sure the bottom of the bowl doesn't touch the water.

Pour the melted chocolate into the prepared tray, tilting it so that it spreads into the corners. While it is still soft, add the toppings of your choice. Leave to set completely at room temperature before breaking into shards.

CHOCOLATE AND BLACK SALT CARAMELS

MAKES ABOUT 64

If you're into making edible gifts or love caramels, these are a winner.
Find briny, mineral-flavoured black salt at health-food shops or
online. Alternatively, use really good plain or smoked sea salt flakes.

150g/5¼oz dark chocolate (50-60%
  cocoa solids), finely chopped or
  grated
400ml/13½fl oz double [heavy]
  cream

400g/14oz granulated sugar
230g/8oz golden [corn] syrup
45g/1½oz unsalted butter
60ml/2fl oz water
black lava salt, to taste

Line a 20×20-cm/8×8-in baking dish with baking paper, making slits in the
corners so that it fits neatly. Let the paper overhang the sides.

Put the chocolate in a heatproof bowl. Heat the cream in a pan until almost
boiling, then pour it over the chocolate and stir until melted and smooth.

Place all the remaining ingredients, except the salt, in a deep, heavy pan. Mix
well so that everything is moistened. Set over a medium-high heat and simmer
without stirring, just swirling the pan now and then, until the temperature
reaches 125°C/257°F on a sugar thermometer. Remove from the heat and very
slowly and carefully pour the chocolate cream into the caramel, stirring all
the time - watch out, as it will froth up. Return to the heat and simmer,
stirring now and then, until the mixture returns to 125°C/257°F. Pour into the
prepared baking dish and leave to cool for 10 minutes. Sprinkle with the salt,
then leave to cool and set at room temperature. This might take a few hours.

When set, lift out using the baking paper as handles onto a chopping [cutting]
board and cut into small squares or rectangles, then wrap in baking paper.
These can be kept for up to 6 months, but don't store in the fridge.

CHOCOLATE AND TAHINI SPREAD

MAKES ABOUT 200ML/6¾FL OZ

This version of chocolate spread is made with tahini, a gloriously unctuous paste produced from ground sesame seeds, and I love the savoury edge it imparts to chocolate. A note about tahini: this recipe works best with a new jar, because the stuff at the bottom of an opened, half-used one tends to be too thick to work well. Ideally, give a new jar a really good stir so that the oil is mixed in and the tahini is lovely and runny. This recipe can - indeed should - be made to your own personal chocolate spread preferences, so add a little more tahini, sugar or cocoa to taste.

200g/7oz tahini
80g/2¾oz icing [confectioners']
  sugar, sifted
50g/1¾oz cocoa powder, sifted

good pinch of sea salt flakes
1-4 Tbsp sesame oil (not toasted),
  as needed

This is less a recipe and more of an assembly job. Place the tahini, icing sugar, cocoa powder and salt in a mixing bowl. Stir by hand or use electric beaters until everything is combined. Slowly beat in enough of the sesame oil to create the consistency of chocolate spread you prefer.

The spread will keep well in a sealed jar for 2 weeks in the fridge.

SWEET DUKKAH

MAKES ABOUT 200G/7OZ

Dukkah is the Egyptian condiment made from nuts, seeds, herbs
and spices, typically used as a dip for bread anointed with olive oil.
This sweet version is equally delicious and versatile: sprinkle it
over yogurt, porridge, stewed fruit or even hot buttered toast.

60g/2¼oz pistachios
60g/2¼oz blanched almonds
2 Tbsp runny honey
75g/2¾oz mixed seeds, including
   sesame seeds
1½ tsp fennel seeds
¼ tsp ground cumin

¼ tsp ground coriander
1 tsp ground cinnamon
1 tsp caster [superfine] sugar
3 Tbsp cacao nibs, roughly crushed
   in a spice or coffee grinder
pinch of sea salt flakes
4 Tbsp dried rose petals

Preheat the oven to 180°C/350°F/Gas mark 4 and line a rimmed baking sheet
with baking paper. Add the pistachios and almonds to the prepared sheet,
drizzle with the honey and stir to coat. Spread out in a single layer and roast
for 10 minutes, or until golden, stirring the nuts halfway through to ensure
even cooking. Keep an eye on the nuts towards the end of the roasting time,
as they will burn easily at this point.

Remove from the oven, lift out the nuts onto the paper and set aside on a
wire rack to cool completely. Once completely cool, pulse in a food processor
to make a rough rubble of finely ground and larger pieces of nuts.

Meanwhile, toast the mixed seeds and fennel seeds in a dry frying pan
until they start to smell toasty. Tip into a bowl and add all the remaining
ingredients, including the blitzed nuts but not the rose petals. Mix well, then
fold in the rose petals. Store in an airtight jar for up to a month.

INDEX

95

Publishing Director: Sarah Lavelle
Senior Commissioning Editor: Céline Hughes
Designers: Claire Rochford & Emily Lapworth
Photographer: Yuki Sugiura
Food Stylist: Aya Nishimura
Prop Stylist: Alexander Breeze
Head of Production: Stephen Lang
Production Controller: Sabeena Atchia

Published in 2022 by Quadrille,
an imprint of Hardie Grant Publishing

Recipes previously published in 2019 by Quadrille in *Cocoa*

Quadrille
52-54 Southwark Street
London SE1 1UN
quadrille.com

Cataloguing in Publication Data: a catalogue record for this book
is available from the British Library.

ISBN 978 1 78713 856 8

Reprinted in 2022 (twice)
10 9 8 7 6 5 4 3

Printed in China